# YARN
*selected poems*

Hughie Carroll

All rights reserved © May 2020

## *Foreword*

A thumbnail sketch of how these words came together. There was a serious accident in 1991 during rehearsals with the now defunct Snapdragon Circus. I was working as a performer with them, juggling, acting, music and stunts, one of which went wrong. There were long-term repercussions in the form of PTSD which eventually morphed into ME. Dealing with this has been hard. Meditation continues to be very helpful, I find. Most of the formal retreat practice I've done has been in the Chinese Chan tradition with the Western Chan Fellowship. Sometimes this process throws up what might be called a 'life review'. The events that really moved me came up to be remembered. Some of them I wrote down.

Taking the 'backward step' in zazen (meditation) I often find that the unconscious gets to work. Moments that seem significant arrange themselves into a haiku/haibun/senryu sort of form, dubbed 'hughku' (thanks, Brendan!). Making them public is taking the 'forward step' of full self-expression, a concept much appreciated from Roshi Reb Anderson. I like to think that together, these two steps are a little dance.

Few people know how long they have here. That fact made me want to document these anecdotes. Here they are in roughly chronological order.

100% true in all details afaik! Email hughie@carrollonline.co.uk.

This book is dedicated with all the love in the world to my little mum.

*Hughie Carroll, 2020*

## *scrabble*

scrabble at Christmas
Grandma Burke visiting
mam and dad in a team
me and Jem

clicking clicky tiles
looking up at the ceiling
making occasional
afcse
cafes
facse
faces

the clock ticked away
intellectual vigour
then suddenly
magnificently
she farted

deeply
sonorously

the adults kept playing
as though Grandma
had not in fact
let one rip
all three
dead straight faces

mine
and Jem's
were pressed into the carpet
belly muscles in spasm
aching cheeks

the more serious they looked
the more we howled
it couldn't
be helped


## *moron*

I have to admit
it was pretty funny
Jem overpowering me
to write in the middle
of my homework

"Sister Mary is a moron"

I stuck some carefully cut paper
over his contribution
and continued my essay
over the top

she discovered the subterfuge
and called me up
in front of the class
it wasn't so funny
being shaken

by the ears


## *bang*

weedkiller and sugar
burned with a supernatural light
a fierce lancing
to the eyes
utterly
fascinating

my brother packed it
into a big glass jar
and made a fuse
out of string

in the lee of a fallen log
I lit that string
the flame wouldn't blow out
to smoulder slowly
but instead raced along
my eleven year old face
inches away

turning to run
at the last second
I remember wheeling
off my feet
the glass hitting my back
whistling past my ears
I was most impressed
that I could briefly make out
a me shaped hole
in the blasting debris

lying on my back
listening to a very high note
my brother called my name

distantly

## *the strap*

a professional maths teacher
asked us
"how many right angles
in the corner of the room?"

the class dutifully responded
"three"
"no, four" she said
and claimed another
"look, right across the ceiling"
me and Kevin protested
"what about the other two walls then?
surely that's six
or even infinity
if you allow that one"

my mistake
was in telling the truth
that she was factually wrong
she demanded silence
and restated
her ridiculous claim

a few days later
filing out of assembly
she noticed my shirt
little pictures
of bicycles or trains or something
a technical infraction
of a little known rule

she sent me for the strap
I waited outside Egen's office
on his way in
I saw him spit
another thing
that would've got us punished

twice he put his back into it
leather across the palm
any semblance of integrity
they believed they had

vanished right then
never to return

## *XTC*

my first proper gig
late seventies
fourteen maybe fifteen years old
XTC at The Affair, Swindon
we used to write
"XTC R NRG"
in the dust on cars
they were the most thrilling thing
to come from that town
they were my connection
to the zeitgeist
me and my mates
put safety pins in our clothes
and tried to punk it up a bit
the band's effect on my nervous system
can't fully be reckoned
the echoes
of the vertiginous excitement
reverberate still
a blast of power
right up close
that's what a Catholic boy needs
raw decibels, invention and pace
to drive out the fakery
the polite suburban dream
exploded

years later
a motley assortment
some original members
including Barry my chum

at his glittering best
wheeled out some of the old tunes
in a packed pub
back in Swindon

they jammed the bit at the end
of 'Making Plans for Nigel'
the bit that repeats
'steel, steel, steel'
the whole crowd sang
shouted
bellowed in unison
'STEEUL, STEEUL, STEEUL'

we were all wrinkly and fat
but that edge was suddenly back
the glee
the remembrance
the heartbreak
the zenith
the tragedy
of a nothing life
in a nothing town
and yet here we were
shoulder to shoulder
dancing
jumping
sweating
singing out
for our lost youth
our refound joy
an exuberant requiem
an ecstatic lament

steel
steel
steel

## *dancing Shiva*

dancing shiva acid
sixteen years old
Stonehenge
surrounded by bikers
hippies and punks
I was fresh from Catholic school
and more than a little
out of my depth

paranoia came like a wave
elemental and overpowering
I locked myself in a car
and whimpered in fright
it peaked and plateaued
as I watched the freaks pass by

a girl held her arm all stiff
as she talked to her companion
that was anxiety
the same that I could feel
and suddenly I realised
we were all in the same boat
we all of us felt fear
a universal tension
brought on by how time
always removes
all the illusions of certainty

my trembling turned to compassion
a vast empathy with the broken
I left the car and floated
possessed by a deity

at some point near the dawn
I changed a baby's nappy

the mum was out cold
and the poor thing was crying
I had never done it before

the sun came up and burned me
my skin is deep sea white
I got naked and covered myself in mud
something I saw in a film
seeing how everyone's minds
where filled with self-concern
I saw how redundant it was
to be self-conscious

and thus at last
I broke out of the suburban dream
primordially in touch
with Mother Earth
and Father Sun

the whole experience marked me
and set my life's course
around that time
I had my ear pierced
and thus the rings remind me
of that ecstatic rite
a journey of tribal allegiance
to what I later learned to call
the Way of the Bodhisattva

## *glassed*

they both weighed
twice as much as me
my rugby mates
I was tough and wiry
but weedy by comparison

we threw the ball about
and each other
until we were sufficiently
muddied
and our clothes
adequately ripped

having worked up a thirst
we ran off to the pub
to further compete
in a royal quaffing
at some point
deep in the ale
one took aim at his head
with an empty pint glass
"one, two" SMASH!
it looked for all the world
like he really had
glassed himself
he had let it go
between "two" and SMASH
it had really just
broken on the floor

the other guy
was also convinced
so he gave it a go
somehow by chance
he only nicked himself
glass all down his chest

"Wow!" thought I
"I didn't know you could do that!"
so "one, two" SMASH!
and I had severed
two arteries in my forehead
as I stood up

I saw two beautiful red jets
spurting
right out in front of me
quickly I was blinded
I grabbed someone
and got them to lead me
outside where they
picked out the glass
I lay my head against a wall
and they pressed against the cuts

the ambulance and the police
arrived pretty soon
a copper rugby tackled
my friend
the one stopping the bleeding
an ambulance man
started berating the policeman
as people streamed
out of the pub
an old nurse took me
by the elbow
and quietly lead me
into an ambulance

dabbing away the blood
just enough to see
I thought I made out
two people locked in combat
rolling out into the road
it had turned
from a fracas
into carnage
as we zipped off
to the hospital

they stitched me up

no anaesthetic
and left me
to sleep it off
at some point in the night
there was an accident
with a bed pan
which was already full

they let me out in the morning
and I stumbled through the rain
an old lady flattened herself
against a wall
to let me past
looking horrified

I glanced at my reflection
in the window of a bustop
covered in piss, blood and mud
clothes tattered
two black eyes
and wires
sticking out of my head
I looked quite a bit
like Frankenstein's monster

## *The Inevitable Split*

the college band
was modelled on Kid Creole
and the Coconuts
1984
Orwell's year

eight of us
different courses
different years

not all in college at all
so we called ourselves
The Inevitable Split

we did tons of gigs
Leeds, Bradford
all over

the best one by far
was at a military place
an amputees recovery unit
only us in the band
not in wheelchairs

a crate of beers
got thrown onto the stage
I tried to remember the chords
as I watched open-mouthed
at them dance

I knew you could balance
on the back wheels
but I didn't know
you could pogo

on one wheel

until it broke

the guy held his stomach
laughing
he got dragged off the dance floor
the broken chair
chucked in a corner
another chair materialised
only to be trashed again

it was like a medieval melee
jousting destruction
they shouted for more
at the end of each song

we belted it out
in awe
at fifty drunken blokes
in hysterics
ripping up
their world

## *groupies*

two girls in the audience
had clearly taken a shine
I played my funky guitar
and tried not to make
eye contact

they seemed enormous
and looked sweaty
something about
their eagerness
and bulk
made me want to run

they waited around
while the band packed up
and I hid
waiting for an opportunity
to bolt

they weren't giving up
and the last of our gear
was about to go

it is a two person job
carrying a bass cabinet
I scooted down behind it
and scuttled along
hoping they wouldn't
see my feet

## *sword*

my old jiu-jitsu teacher
used to have a short sword
its blade milled off
it was used occasionally in class
it was from Korea
and had been used
in World War II
so we were told

there were loads of cool things
that we learned all about
the stances and cuts
the formal defences
this was some of the actual stuff
the Samurai would learn

I borrowed it for a while
to practice at home
once the teacher trusted me enough

back in my room I studied it
having the time and quiet
and found seven notches
right up by the hilt

I began to think what they meant
and reality came to stay

I couldn't sleep
with it there in the room
it gave me a cold shiver
I no longer thought it cool
and gave it right back
at the earliest opportunity
I had come to see
that we had kind of been playing
on the bones

of the dead

## *Joanne Whalley*

they were filming Edge of Darkness
at the Ilkley College Student Union
I showed up to get some chips
and wondered why there was
cables and tech stuff everywhere
in the canteen
there sat a woman
the most preternaturally
ethereally
beautiful creature
I had ever seen
in my whole entire life
after a few questions
some chums lent me
a notepad
so I approached her
Joanne Whalley
in the glory of youth
saying I was a reporter
for the college rag
I bought her a coffee
and wrote down

what she said
but I wasn't really listening
having already drowned
in her eyes


## *2 Hot 4 July*

the only band on the island
2 Hot 4 July
we had a special gig
in the ancient Greek amphitheatre

I was furious with the leader
he hadn't paid us tuppence
all his promises
like his Jamaican accent
turned out to be fake

my song was Psycho Killer
when I took the main mic
for the guitar solo
I made like Jimi Hendrix
leaving the thing
on the stage
with broken strings
and feedback screaming
the starry vault above
torn in half
by the ecstatic howl

afterwards a man came up
he claimed to have signed Madonna
he asked me to send him a tape
but I had no songs of my own
and somehow lost his address

## *body-builders*

a beach bar in Greece
a gang of bronzed
German body-builders
it was my round
and as I headed to the bar
their ring leader
cracked some joke about me
they looked up
at my pale scrawny body
and all roared with laughter

a classic moment
almost the proverbial
sand kicked in my face

but then I thought
of all the nationalities there
from all over the world
it wasn't ok to laugh at their skin
my skin was from my ancestors
they were laughing at them
seized by an unexpected rage
I stared at their boss
his gang
one by one
noticed me glaring
and broke off laughing
to look down at the floor

at last their leader noticed
his gang not backing him up
his smile suddenly gone
I lifted my fists in victory
the whole bar erupted
in applause

## *white hats*

people kept warning me
about the white hat police
on Naxos

the last busker
the previous summer
had his banjo
bust over his head
and had been
jailed

doing a show
on the waterfront
there was a sizeable crowd
forming a circle
four or five deep

it was going well
everyone having fun
suddenly some shouting
two white hats
burrowing through the audience

my hat was full of drachmas
I yammed it on my head
the people behind me parted
so I could leg it
round the corner

peeking carefully back
the police had got to the centre
the circle had closed around them
it looked like folks were expecting
the next performance

a striptease maybe?
expressive dance?

## *finale*

street juggling finale
looking straight up
throwing those balls so high
I didn't see the kid
romper suit
reins trailing
wobble out of the crowd
and punch me

right in the doodads

as I hit the floor
the demon returned
to its parents
as my juggling things
landed on me
and I tried
not to be sick

it was the biggest laugh
I ever got

## *3 minutes*

the clowning workshop
could really get rough
away for a week
with some scary genius
at one point
we had to go on stage

for a timed three minutes
we were not allowed
to move or speak

at first there was panic
self-consciousness at its worst
it felt like something pressing
hard up against my face
a thing I had been avoiding
for as long as I could remember

the thing is
anxiety can only go so high
and then it can't maintain itself
and naturally begins to drop
the pressure eased off
I noticed someone in the audience
and they noticed me
noticing them
for some reason it was funny
and people began to giggle
pretty soon it was riotous
I'm still not really sure
just what was so funny
but my God, funny it was!

my three minutes was up
I felt like a king
never again did stage fright
come to spoil the party


## *Eisteddfod*

me and Peewee were put on last
then the compere went home
so our slot became open ended

no one to stop us

a largish crowd
three or four hundred
in rows of seats
in a semi-permanent hall
in a park in central Cardiff

we improvised from the start
and things became wild
at one point I climbed the rafters
over the audience's heads
no safety of any kind
that was kind of the point

the audience went with us
the Lords of Misrule
the children's reactions
being the main source of fun

at one point I asked
"Ok kids, who wants to be
DECAPITATED?"
a forest of hands went up
Peewee explained
all the glory details
while I went hunting
for a plausible implement of doom

I returned with a table leg
and Peewee had our victim
a sweet young girl
on her knees
hands behind her back
head bowed
and apparently willing to die
in the name of entertainment

the adult part of the crowd
had turned into a mob
something atavistic
had curiously seized
this celebration
of all things Welsh

things went all the way
right up to the point
where I only had two options
carry out a brutal bludgeoning
or ask for the applause
the young girl in question
took several
curtain calls


## *necrophilobats*

acrobalance
I think it's called
Peewee would get knocked
in the head
'die'
and get rigor mortis
he could then be moulded
into a base
Kim would balance on him
upside down
pretty nifty

I played the swanee whistle
for drama
a touch of mockery
and gave a facetious commentary

I changed it one day

ad-libbing
"jadies and mentlemen
watch as an acrobat
turns into
a necrophilobat"

now it's potentially dangerous
upside down and everything
but watching the two of them
trying to keep it together
while having hysterics
was profoundly pleasing
especially since
it took
some time

## *chocolate*

long distance club passing
the final
European Juggling Convention
Maastricht 1989

I had teamed up
with Pete the Punk
he had a smile
that warmed from a distance
we were up against
legends
the hot favourites
Haggis and Lee

someone must've nobbled them
somehow they went down
and we won

the prizes were Dutch chocolate
made into juggling clubs
a whole pound of it
each

flushed with success
we entered the three legged race
whilst juggling of course
I remember it being funny
but now how we fluked it
winning that one too

another wee ceremony
another two clubs
making four pounds
of Dutch chocolatey darkness
to smash up
and distribute
a process that took
seconds

## *giraffes*

it might've been Llanelli
or somewhere just like it
me and Seb did a show
at a shopping centre

we had giraffe unicycles
and the help
of a grumpy security guard
the natural enemy
of the street performer

I remember the enjoyment
of making him carry

some of our stuff
making him look
like part of the show
his suppressed fury
made me happy
a sweet sweet revenge

Seb discovered he could hover
on the five foot uni
onto the walkalator
that went up
to the second floor
he made it to the top
a death defying feat
and received a tremendous
round of applause

the obvious thing
was for me to try it too
he came down
as I went up
high fiving
in the middle

the entire shopping centre
at a standstill
hovering
without security

## *wind*

we had been climbing
all day long
the wind at the top
was steady
as a rock

the routes were shortish
I spent a fair amount of time
bringing in the ropes
leaning on that wind
so strong

right at the last
before going home
we went to look over
and say goodbye

the angle we stood at
put the eyes level with the rim
and the feet about
a foot back
appropriately enough

I don't know what possessed me
but I inched forward
so the toes
got to the lip
the eyes looked back
onto the headwall

nearer to flight
I couldn't get
a snatched moment
delirious
eternal

oh but you could lean
on that wind

was it an act of faith
or tempting fate?

## *Dobra*

Nick had told me
about the Dobra Valley
how no one had ever gone down it
and come out alive
how he had tried by himself
a few years previously
how close he'd come
to starving
during an epic escape
he needed a chum
so down we went

we had ropes
supplies
training
but the first big challenge
was a waterfall
way taller than our ropes
we picked our way
down the side
hundreds of metres
of scree
one false move
and pfft

after that we were committed
neither of us imagining
we could go back up
so on we went
after some nosh
and bravado

the valley narrowed
there was time
for photos

so we thought
but the river disappeared
around a bend
between vertical walls

it was hard to choose
but we swam

stupid

the rucksack took me under
should've taken it off
there was not enough strength
to get back to the surface
as my breath gave out
he hauled me up
by the scruff of the neck
and there I was
worrying about another waterfall
beyond that bend

both of us scared
and exhausted
we forced our way on
down a broadening valley
at one point seeing
human footprints
our eyes always craning upwards
for any possible escape
the sun dipped low

the walls narrowed again
water quicker
blacker
another bend
we both knew
we were not going to make it

not this time

we backtracked
feeling desperate
but there
in the failing light
we saw a barn
way up high
that had to be an escape

forcing through brambles
heaving steep and loose
scrabbling up moss
it was night
by the time we flopped
over a little wall
into a meadow
we laughed and cried
with relief
the little cabana
would have a loft
full of straw
we could sleep in

a bull

yes a bull
came to have a look
it pawed the ground
tossing its head
just like a cartoon
my last bit of adrenaline
sped my wobbling legs
over to the barn

I looked back
to see how Nick was getting on

he sat where I left him
the bull bellowed
but Nick bellowed back

"FUCK

OFF!"

to my astonishment
it did

after a night of space-blankets
shivering
dehydration
blood-loss
and straw beasts
nibbling at us
we hitched back to our base
the local Guardia Civil
were surprised to see us
having told everyone
that the last two people
to give it a go
had never returned

## *leather jacket*

that leather jacket
kinda saved my life

stepping off the train
in Sowerby Bridge
I shivered
a half snow
had come
to kill

huddling through the market
I saw prominently displayed
a rock & roll jacket
red on the shoulders
red on the elbows
all beat up
but lined and warm

a sticker on it
said £10
so I rummaged through my pockets
a night out in Bradford
at my chum's place
chess, beer, spliffs
and I was a bit hungover
and worried about no dinner
the circus tour
had left me skint
and threadbare

there!
a tenner!
hang the dinner
the jacket won hands down
winter
won't be sniffed at

back at the bus
my folks had sent a letter
inside
was a tenner


## *red faces in the park*

Finchley Fair had asked
for a contribution from the circus

so a bunch of us piled in a van
we were only down the road

that morning a Minister
after an anti-German rant
had been forced to resign

guessing the iron lady
might put in an appearance
Finchley being Thatcher's constituency
we learned the tune
to the beautiful old hymn
"Deutschland Deutschland
uber alles"
they changed the words now

I was on trumpet
and could only just about
hold the tune
the sax and trombone
were real proper pros
and did all the glorious harmonies

when we got there
dotted about
were heavy set guys in suits
with earpieces
sharp haircuts
and bulges under their arms
"Thatcher's coming isn't she?"
but they wouldn't answer

ten minutes later
suddenly there she was
a surreal pantomime dame
she rocketed around in a circuit
surrounded by heavies

so
1, 2, 3, 4
we played the tune

a local guy leaned over
and bonked the end of my trumpet
loosening my front teeth
moments later she was gone

the Sun reporter was beside himself
delirious with joy
hopping from foot to foot
he took our details
and sure enough
the next day
in that apalling rag
"Red Faces in the Park"
a tiny article appeared
"Cheeky clowns
embarrassed the premier
after Ridley's resignation"

a bruised lip
was a very small price
for such a deep satisfaction

## *Tel Aviv TV*

"quick quick grab your costume
we'll explain on the way"
Israeli fixers with radios
hustled me into a jeep
"they need someone from your circus
to be interviewed and to perform
so that's you – COME ON
the plane is already waiting"

the dust flew up we sped along
and skidded to a stop
at the airport
more people with radios
waving us through
we ran through the building
and out on to the runway
the plane looked like the one
at the end of Casablanca

a soldier let me have
his window seat
"I've seen it before"
he pointed out the Sea of Galilee
Nazareth, Bethlehem
I held back tears
we saw the golden dome
way over in Jerusalem
I was lost
in astonishment
the plane came to Tel Aviv
and wheeled out over the sea
and back to land
suddenly I was on the pavement
no on there to meet me

I twiddled my thumbs
feeling like a lemon
until a car zoomed up
"Oh God, we're sorry!
there's been a mistake
the TV studios are shut today.
How about some shopping?
Your plane back
is this afternoon"

I wandered around

found a nice necklace
and bought it for my girlfriend
I tried to haggle in Hebrew
having learned "one" to "ten"
the guy spit out his toothpick laughing
slapped his thighs
and called his friend out
they said they admired "chutzpah"

back at the airport
I joined the queue
to check in bags and guns
an enormous man in front of me
pulled out this massive cannon
silver
amazing
from a holster under his arm
it sounded like a typewriter
when he clunked it down

my turn came
they opened my suitcase
and pulled out some beanbags
two ping pong balls
some rizla papers
they guy hefted a juggling club
with a look of sheer contempt
it looked like he was thinking
"how could you kill someone
with that?"

back in Eilat at twilight
I was bunged back in a jeep
"quick quick the show is about to start"
again the dust and speeding
this time past a huge crowd
my brain was already overloaded

but it was suddenly time
to step out and go to the mic
"erev tov kahal nichbad"
(good evening honourable audience)
8000 people cheering
really knocks your socks off

the show went ok
apart from some dayglo paint
accidentally poured
on my hand and in my eye
just before I was supposed
to juggle

the excitement of that day
faded all too fast
but that night over beers
I thought it would last
forever

## *library*

the book had the title
"Speed Reading"
in big bold letters on the cover
I slid it across the desk

the librarian was large
an example of what
used to be called
"matronly"

she went through the rigmarole
of cards and ink and stamps
thonk! thonk!
and slid it back

I riffled the pages with my thumb
thrrrrip!
and sliding it back once more
said "thanks very much"

she froze in her clumpy shoes
and gave me a look
Lucifer himself
would have been impressed
a look of winter
of savage contempt
of something beyond the grave

I felt that dreadful gaze on my back
as I speedily withdrew
my giggles forced down into silence
back outside
I think my laughter bursting out
was accompanied
by a tiny drop
of wee

## *snapdragon before*

so exciting
to winch up the king poles
they held up the little big top
for Snapdragon Circus

they head hunted me
to be in the show
I was thrilled to bits
1990 and so called 'new circus'
was all the rage

the king poles were held in place

by a big heavy cable
sledge-hammered into the ground
with two enormous stakes
that first time for me
putting the tent up
was like dreaming

I climbed one of the poles
during a break for tea and cigs
looking around
from way up top
I realised it was
"a moment"
a redolent pause
where the scene was set
the characters introduced
all the drama
about to begin

that beautiful blonde girl
big bouncy barky dog
old green Bedford bus
I was about to properly fall
head over heels in love

musicians and children
acrobats and actors
technicians and weirdos
artistes and fools
tightrope, jugglery, costumes
all laid out below me
relaxing

the show was basically theatre
my character an outsider
who keeps stopping the action
on some administrative pretence

the ring master's magic powers
would trick Mr Gasket
into performing various stunts
against his will and in a trance
until finally he wakes up
and changes his mean old ways
and runs away with the circus
of his own free will

that tour
that summer
was the absolute best time
a boy can possibly have
some hundred shows
around the UK
and finishing in Israel
representing the country
The International Festival of New Circus
but we were still only really
just a bunch of hippies

follow your dreams
everyone says
but what happens
when they become

nightmares?

## *snapdragon during*

rehearsals
Sowerby Bridge
13th April 1991

we were speeding up the stunt
that had been going so well

the whole year before
me on the stage
hands in straps
rope up to a pulley
across to a second pulley
and down to two people
high up in the netting
when they jumped
I would fly up fast
the audience would freak
as I hit the roof above their heads

my mate's feet were hurting
from hitting the ground
the rope was shortened
no one thought it through
he would now take the weight
on his hands
so down he went
his hands pulled free
I no longer had
a counter balance

I hit the rigging bar
way too hard
everything much too fast
my body went horizontal
and then time went weird
dilated
looking at my clothes
all blue with red bumper boots
seemed to go on and on
just hanging there
all weightless
and utterly certain
that nothing in this world

was going to stop me falling
all the way way down
to that hard hard stage

next thing I saw myself
from over on the empty seating
long enough to think both
"oh, so that's what I look like"
and
"what the FUCK am I doing over here?"

then

the abyss

no light anywhere
no stars
no world
no body
just a point of consciousness
in an infinite void
I don't have the language
to get it across
words like "terror" and "fear"
just point in the right direction
and that was only the start

after a while it became clear
that if I went to my right
I would re-enter my body
that was where all the pain was
so I didn't want to do that
then if I went to my left
I would never again
be back inside my body
and just stay in that void
alone forever

you can't die if you have no body

it felt like maybe twenty minutes
I floated in that dread
until I thought my point of awareness
would fly apart with stress
an arm came around me
"come with me Hughie, it's ok"
and it whizzed me
through immense distances
at bewildering speed
and put me
exquisitely gently
back inside my body
between my shoulder blades
the single most painful moment
of my life

## *snapdragon after*

they said I had 90% bruising
and that I would be ok
after about three months
I rejoined the circus
after only a fortnight
and re-wrote my part
removing all the physical stuff
and focused on acting
and music

I was struggling to understand
just what had happened
things were just not right
they did not seem real
everyone carried on
just like before

apparently unaware
of the presence of death
like two great dark wings
the dragon hovered silent
and I felt my body falling
but strangely never landing
from time to time on stage
even while delivering lines
I would suddenly see myself
from behind my right shoulder
and became increasingly confused
about whether I had survived
my body certainly didn't belong
so I wasn't sure where I was
even while taking
the audience's applause

in zazen I found a way
the only thing that worked
holding awareness on the body
allowing chaotic feelings
and trying not to flinch

today is an anniversary
twenty eight years
since I was brought back
twenty eight years
of trying to work out why
there has to be some reason
for such a miracle
it can't just be
punishment can it?
the daily pain and exhaustion
has been such a burden
but it has propelled me
on the Buddhist path

I remember asking the fates
if they would accept me
as an initiate
to take the wisdom road
so I have to take responsibility
and accept reality
just the way it is

at least one thing's for sure
and that is a matter of attitude
if I'm asking 'what love do I get?'
then the suffering is terrible
if I'm asking 'what love do I give?'
then everywhere seems filled
with ordinary magic

## *the ferryman*

the human body
is not supposed to survive
a twenty seven foot fall
onto the back
on a hard surface
so the consultant said

"you should break the skull
and the spine and rupture
the internal organs
that none of these three things
have happened
I frankly have no explanation for
young man!"

he looked sharply over
half moon glasses
he wore a three piece suit

and I think belonged
in the 1950s

so if I shake or cry
or need yet another nap
don't think
"there's something wrong with him"

because there isn't

it's just the fare for the ferryman
to bring me back across
just what Mother Nature needs
in return
for my life

## *endarkenment*

my endarkenment was total
an absence of light
and also of matter
both internal and external

bodiless

I hung suspended
in an infinite abyss

decades later
the dread of it
still clings about me
but that experience
was actually a defence
the brainstem functioning
to protect me
from the savage reality

of the impact of the fall

just like a nightmare
recalled in the daytime
it can still give a jolt
but it can be known
as a strangeness
an illusion
unreal
something from the beyond

so when my nervous system
goes into the old trauma
and everything is demanding
to bolt like a horse
again and again
I must reassure myself
that it's all a false alarm
that really there is no crisis
that the past really has gone
and in the present
I am safe
that the universe does want me
the proof of which
is that right now

I am here

## *Romanians*

my friend had a gig near me
and invited me along
an East European rugby squad
was about to play England
at Twickenham

my mate did stand-up comedy
they absolutely loved it
they were out from behind
the iron curtain
for the first time in their lives

at one point a deal was done
their vodka for my dope
a super strong charras
you had to handle with care

the following evening
my friend rang me
"look at the results"
our new friends
had set a record
losing
54 – 3


## *arrested*

in the mid 90s
I had a garret room
the landlord was away
London
IT
a summer hot spell
he asked me to water
his grass plants

before dawn
loud banging
at the door
three storeys below

coppers in tracksuits

demanded to be let in
there was more of them
round the back
climbing over garages
looking purposeful

I was loaded into a van
along with a dozen plants
me and a bored policeman
took in the aroma
until the rest of them
were satisfied
that there was in fact
no drugs factory
their tip-off
was false

they took me to the cells
removed laces
belt
and left me alone
around 5am

not so different
from zen retreat
thought I
and cobbled together
a meditation cushion

I assumed the position

size 16 footsteps
along the corridor
a slot slid open
a pen clicked
something ticked
a slot slid back

footsteps louder
the cell next to mine
a slot slid open
a pen clicked
something ticked
a slot slid back

footsteps louder still
my cell
a slot slid open
"oh!"
a slot slid back
footsteps hurried away

muffled conversation
then returning
two pairs of feet
a slot slid open
more muffled conversation
some surprise
some laughter
a slot slid back

they were incredibly
apologetic
when they eventually
let me go
"It's not exactly
the great train robbery"
they said
dissappointed
as they handed me
my stuff

## *the golden fleece*

all the gear fell out
as I started the crux
of the golden fleece
at Symonds Yat
looking down the rope
eighty odd feet or so
all the protection
I'd put in
popped

my brother looked up
helpless to help me

I could've tried reversing
but that looked dodgy
the headwall didn't look too hard
being scared
would only make a fall
more likely

the mind
stopped
the moves
flowed

two minutes
of simplicity
of flight

of accidental

perfection

## *El Naranjo de Bulnes*

the picture says it all kind of

there I sit on the summit
of that wondrous mountain
1989 "I ran the world" t-shirt
wearing my boina
in the majesty of youth
relaxed
triumphant
an effortless smile

even when it was being taken
I knew it was both literally
and metaphorically
a high point

fast forward twelve years
my then wife
her struggles with low confidence
and me
my struggles with PTSD
on the summit again

in that second picture
you can kind of tell
she really isn't happy
to be there

I thought it would be
a symbolic triumph
for both of us
but the effort of getting her up
added to the even greater effort
of getting her back down
sort of did for me

our last abseil was in the dark
strangers helped us back to camp
everything I had
had been spent
in helping, encouraging, cajoling
sometimes sheer lifting
a person whose fear
had turned her into luggage

a few days later
back at work
on my way back from the toilet
between one footfall and another
I felt a pang
I thought it was flu
that was the moment
that all 'that' started
the endless treadmill
of ME
the overexertion
on top of the fall
was something the system
just could not abide
the brakes went on
and all these years later
they simply will not
come off


## *leg*

one snowy Christmas
the whole family went
to the woods
I had a wrestle
with my brother
both of us

middle-aged
it seemed the perfect opportunity
to spring some jiu-jitsu
I waited for him to push
and spun around
for a hip throw
the inner edge of my boot
had caught in the snow
leaving my foot behind
pop pop
and my leg was broke
dad drove me to the hospital
there was a long wait
he leaned over to whisper
see that guy?
he's come in
to have his tie
straightened

## *chess*

the scars were deep
all over his face
car windscreen maybe?
we sat down
shook hands
arranged the pieces
set the clock
and began
the cut
and thrust
gradually
the nerves subsided
and eventually
I set a trap
a pawn as bait

to tempt his queen
once in
she was doomed
in three moves
at most
the permutations
branched out
like broccoli
at the end
each flower
was death
I checked it
over and over
and made my move
heart in mouth
attention shifted
to him
his eyes brightened
noticing
his prey
his spirits lifted
as he thought it
undefended
I could read his mind
on his battered face
feel his joy rising
as he reached out
and took it
over the next few moves
the reality dawned
his features crumbled
his demeanour sank
his life
drained out
my guilt
lacerating

taking his queen
another cut

## *bucket*

over the doctor's shoulder
I hallucinated Green Tara
ethereal light all around
she winked at me
and I smiled
"yes, please yes, I'm ready"
but I wasn't
or she wasn't
and the doctor found a vein

later he said it was
his personal best
bringing someone back
from that far gone
I remember him telling
the little Indian boy
to run

fast

to get the list of medical things
he'd just given him

I had started feeling sick
just after breakfast
and quickly lost many litres
of body fluids
from both ends
I was staying in a monastery
in Bodh Gaya
and in my cell

rupturing my life
into a bucket
I was trying to raise the alarm
but then kept passing out
this cycle
went around and around
for two or three hours
before someone heard me

an English doctor
months later
said it was most likely
cholera
Christ on a bike! cholera!
well
another close call I guess

from that I know
that I'm not afraid to die
it's to be alone forever
in that infinite void
that's what grips me
the utter cold panic
frozen isolation
a desolation so complete
the Queen of the Dead herself
would turn away
in fright


## *sapphire*

the taxi driver
kept taking me to shops
carpets, suits, jewellery
all over Chennai
it got boring

one place had a glass case
with bright lights
and incredible sapphires
I asked to see one

the guy unlocked it
and took out a cushion
with the biggest glittery rock
I'd ever seen
a blue that sliced
and thrilled

he handed it to me
I took it
my hand forming the starting position
for the 'French Drop'
the simplest sleight of hand
and 'boff' it was gone
I couldn't help it

reaching over
I pulled it out of his ear
and gave it back
but he'd already pressed the alarm

two big heavies
materialised out of thin air
like genies
and frogmarched me out
laughing
helplessly

me
not them

## *scattering*

they had come to the island
to scatter the ashes
daughter
son-in-law
husband

about to leave Thailand
and not yet found
a fitting time and place
to fulfil
the dead woman's
last wishes

the beach she named
had turned into
a scuba resort
bars
music
hedonism
I had just come from a monastery
yells
bells
smells

a chance encounter
led to an impromptu service
at first light
we had a little fire
we had incense
and chanting
time for people
to say their bit
to remember
to cry

it came to the part
where she poured out
grey remains powdered
a life in the surf

this daughter returned
she laughed and cried
at the same time
I felt the aching heart
of the world
embracing everything

## *Grist*

I had asked him
not to leave
his liturgy on the floor
that's what we called
the sheets of A4
that had our Dharma words
the things to say and chant
at the start and the end
of our weekly meditation group
he had come for years
but very on and off
spending months or longer
seriously on the piss

he busked the guitar in town
and was borderline homeless
when he was sober
he would go back to running
he had represented his county
at hurdles I think it was

something about my request

made him proper crazy
he jumped to his feet
and thrust his face into mine
"it's only a piece of paper"
he barked
as he flapped it hard
on the ground once more

I don't recall my response
probably tried to be diplomatic
what I do recall is the obituary
a few years later
he had chucked himself
under a train

it said he had six times
the normally fatal dose
of alcohol in his blood
at the time

I feel sure the two are related
the disrespect and the death
but somehow it now feels wrong
even to speculate
except to say
I now feel
the meaning of the words
is in the manner of their handling


## *Bott*

in the IT office
childish geeky banter
if someone left their computer
unwisely unlocked
someone would jump on

and send a message

"I love the cock!"

how we laughed

one night it snowed
boy did it snow
the buses were cancelled
me and my chum
crunched in on foot
during the slog and sparkle
we hatched a plan
most dastardly

an adjacent car park
was lower than our office
so there we went
and side by side
in four foot tracks
we spelled out
a message for our friend
the esteemed Mr Bott

"Bott (heart symbol) cock"

brilliant
we sniggered
and went back to work

our esteemed colleague
had taken a photo
and sent it to a mate
in fun
someone in head office
had overseen it
and that afternoon

a boss barked

"who wrote it?"
I owned up

he gave me a dressing down
I offered to take the hit
and get sacked
if he let my co-conspirator
off the hook

later still
he had the same conversation
with the other miscreant

"I'm Spartacus!"
we had both said

the snow melted
eventually away
into legend

## *levitation*

there is a levitation trick
we're not supposed to tell
how it's done
like most magic
the secret
is disappointing

returning from the bathroom
to my brand new girlfriend's
bedroom
it was all bedecked
with candles

with not a stitch on
I realised
the setting was perfect
so I went into character
walked very slowly
seriously
silently
to the end of the bed

in a solemn gesture
of finger to lips
I asked for her quiet
and total attention

after a dramatic pause
I lifted
a handswidth
off the floor
and floated
for an impossible
heartbeat

I managed to keep the mood
dead serious
as I took both her hands
in mine
and gazing into
her big round eyes
made her promise
breathlessly
that she would never tell
a living soul
what exactly
she had just witnessed

never good at deadpan
I must've laughed

for half an hour

so if you can keep
a secret
well

so can I


## *shine*

dreaming of my grandma
and mam
baking in the kitchen

I asked where brother number 4 was
"he's taking number 2 swimming"
said my mam

"but how can the younger one
take the older one?"
I asked

"haven't you heard?
the families turned
upside down
now the younger
looks after the older"

"but I'm the youngest
how can I look after
everyone?"

grandma looks up
and says
"all you have to do

is shine!"

## Gaumin Si

outside the Chan hall
at Gaumin Si
we discussed and stretched
after De Lin's Dharma talk
I told John I thought
one of the best bits
was when he said
"the silence of silent illumination
is not the silence of no thoughts
it's the silence of no reaction"
John poked me in the forehead

"don't

you

forget it!"


## Tiananmen Square

Tiananmen square
just leaving
a pair of synchronised soldiers
in high camp paraded
super quick right past us
I think they were wearing
actual makeup
John said "not like
in the British army"
I said "by the left
MINCE!"
and we wiggled our
bums and flounced
right under the nose

of a very cross looking
bulldog of a guard
I think I actually injured
some intercostal muscles
we laughed so hard
Ah John
zen master clowning
that's what I salute


## *lynch mob*

how hard is it
to make a music video?
I was thinking
doing an experiment
stepping very slowly
meditatively
towards the main drag
holding my phone
up by my chest

I'd speed it up
so the walking was normal
everyone else very fast

if I hadn't stopped filming
I could've shown you
the woman running up
the red face
the spit flying out
the jabbing finger
the volume

"IT'S ILLEGAL TO FILM CHILDREN!"
she shrieked
I looked around

but saw no one
turning back
I said "wh?"
but she was off again

"YOU SHOULD BE ASHAMED!"
"IT'S DISGRACEFUL!"
and so forth
she power marched away
I fled into a shop
to buy a sandwich
and to wait for my heart
to slow down

as I got back
to where I was working
I heard a banging on windows
there she was again
on a passing bus
accusing finger
pointing right at me
surrounded by a mob of blokes
lots of tattoos
not much hair

happy shoppers
become
lynch mob


## *mist*

flying my blue motorbike
over that big old bridge to Wales
into an enfoldment of mist

nearly blind

I slowed to a near stall

over the hump
descending
a lorry came up behind
flashing lights
honking

lifting the helmet's visor
I saw that the cloud
was left behind
except for a little bubble
all mine

## *models*

the lorry arrived
one thousand CDs
my album
was here

a bunch of us
ran down the stairs
the guy rolled up a shutter
hefted out one of the boxes
one hundred copies

excitement built up
negotiating cardboard
flaps and folds
then there it was
Mantrasphere

the printing looked ok
there was fiddly cellophane
and everything

an actual real album
at last

the first copy
I gave to the driver
a sort of good luck ritual
he accepted with a sniff
made me sign a form
and got gone

there was a party
a few weeks later
a programmer friend
turned fashion photographer
had a bunch of models
over for a house party

it snowed
I skidded
mostly sideways
grimly determined to make it
whatever the damage
after all
you never knew
we might get snowed in
and now I was
a genuine
bona fide
recording artist

it might have a Buddhist theme
but I ain't
no monk

## *finger ring*

wedding gig
doing magic
for the bridesmaids

"this is a finger ring
good isn't it!?
do you like that?
everyone likes
a good finger ring
don't they?!"

the kind of naughty line
that has to be handled carefully

on this occasion
a guy was about to swallow
a mouthful of champagne
and managed to snort it

we all watched
transfixed
as he heroically struggled
to not let it
explode out of his nose

when at last he swallowed
tears down his cheeks
everyone jumped to their feet
for a standing ovation


## *Paul Daniels*

a tweet offered a place
a Paul Daniels Master Class
twelve would-be magicians

to spend a day
at his house
I answered and got it
the last place
the last minute

he answered the door
a beautiful house
near a village
called Wargrave
I looked down
he really was
that small

Debbie McGee made coffee
I was filled with a sense
of the surreal
we waited for the others
with a tongue tied guy
paralysed with nerves

they rang to say
they had broken down
so the three of us
started without them
they never did
show up

before she left us
Debbie warned us
he could talk forever
when we had had enough
we had to say so

there were two big white rabbits
in an enormous cage
and bizarre magical paraphernalia

in every corner

in the toilet there were photos
of the great man posing
with all the political figures
I detested

he started with all business
how to make a living
all the tricks
of making money
he told us of his poverty
claiming he was eleven
when he saw his first tree
the industrial North East
sounded like Mordor
it started to make sense
his allegiance
to those who charm and trick
so the rich get richer
bugger the rest

he was hilarious
and brilliant
amazing us
every few minutes
our silent partner
leaving the conversation
to just me
and the grandee

there was an endless stream
of incredible anecdotes
he had known
anyone famous
for over fifty years
my favourite

was about the Prince of Dubai
who he had entertained
without props or preparation
when the hired magician
another famous name
had managed to offend
Paul had disappeared
everything off the banquet table
piece
by piece

after the third racist joke
1970s style
and vile
he said
"you can't tell jokes like that anymore"
I said
"there's a reason for that Paul"
there was a frosty silence
but he forgave me
and pointed towards his neighbour's house
around the bend of the river
it belonged to the spoon bender
Uri Geller
Paul said the river
used to be straight

he challenged me
to vanish something
I used his own method
slightly ashamed
to ingratiate

he gave up his secrets
in such a sweet way
I could tell that he liked me
he told a story

of someone offering hundreds of pounds
waving the cash around
for a trick
but he didn't give it up
because he didn't like him
he then went on to show me
I felt blessed

at one point I asked him
about the Mrs Merton joke
she had asked Debbie McGee
"what first attracted you
to millionaire Paul Daniels?"
a crack that has lasted
the one everyone seems to remember
he was clearly wounded
and said that the irony
was that it was Debbie
who was the rich one
when they first met

some months later
we went to his show
at the Wyvern Theatre
at the meet and greet
afterwards
he recognised me
we smiled
so complicated
that acknowledgement
I liked him
not a lot
but I liked him

it was among
his last few shows

shortly afterwards
he disappeared

## *scroll*

I'd been asked
to talk on Chan
at the Ashmolean
there was a calligrapher there
Bing Nan Li
he had no English

a group milled about
I decided to begin
and called their attention
with a bell
and chanting

when I sang
the ancient tunes
the three refuges
the four great vows
the traditional Chinese
he came close and sat
I sensed his emotion
in his demeanour

after my talk
a noise
about silence
the translator
came to tell me
the man had decided
to give me a scroll
the Heart Sutra
she was

consternated
saying the artefact
was precious

not feeling worthy
I put that aside
and accepted
whatever the gesture meant
to him
was a mystery
not to be
evaluated

## *airborne*

all the stories my dad told
about his time down the mines
the "coal tattoo" behind his ear
from when he was knocked
unconscious

when my new father in law
at the head of the table
declared "of course everyone
was behind Thatcher,
unless you were a miner, haha"

my blood boiled
as it must

a few minutes later
my new mother in law
Cruella
sprang to her cloven hooves
and shaking a finger
right in my face

pretty much yelled
"African countries are poor
because they are LAZY!"

I'm glad I lost my temper
slamming my fist on the table
"I'M NOT HAVING IT!"

all the crockery
was just for a moment

airborne

## *rain*

floundering through the labyrinth
the hostile environment
after months
the benefits interview
arrived

the lady was nice enough
but the grilling
was gruelling
my disabilities laid bare

each question
uncovering
exposing
unpleasant truths

my brave face slipped off
as I left
rain lashed down
diagonal drenching
the nadir

all mixed
with tears

a hollow laugh
at the cliche

## *Index*

| | |
|---|---|
| scrabble | 5 |
| moron | 6 |
| bang | 6 |
| the strap | 7 |
| XTC | 9 |
| dancing Shiva | 11 |
| glassed | 12 |
| The Inevitable Split | 15 |
| groupies | 17 |
| sword | 18 |
| Joanne Whalley | 19 |
| 2 Hot 4 July | 20 |
| body-builders | 21 |
| white hats | 22 |
| finale | 23 |
| 3 minutes | 23 |
| Eisteddfod | 24 |
| necrophilobats | 26 |
| chocolate | 27 |
| giraffes | 28 |
| wind | 29 |
| dobra | 31 |
| leather jacket | 34 |
| red faces in the park | 35 |
| Tel Aviv TV | 37 |
| library | 40 |
| snapdragon before | 41 |
| snapdragon during | 43 |
| snapdragon after | 46 |
| the ferryman | 48 |
| endarkenment | 49 |
| Romanians | 50 |
| arrested | 51 |
| the golden fleece | 54 |
| El Naranjo de Bulnes | 55 |
| leg | 56 |
| chess | 57 |
| bucket | 59 |
| sapphire | 60 |
| scattering | 62 |
| Grist | 63 |
| Bott | 64 |
| levitation | 66 |
| shine | 68 |
| Gaumin Si | 69 |
| Tiananmen Square | 69 |
| lynch mob | 70 |
| mist | 71 |
| models | 72 |
| finger ring | 74 |
| Paul Daniels | 74 |
| scroll | 79 |
| airborne | 80 |
| rain | 81 |

● *To see more of Hughie Carroll's work, visit carrollonline.uk*

Lightning Source UK Ltd.
Milton Keynes UK
UKHW021832260720
367213UK00003B/39

9 781715 199692